The Complete Wedding Music Planner

AMSCO PUBLICATIONS
PART OF THE MUSIC SALES GROUP
LONDON / NEW YORK / PARIS / SYDNEY / COPENHAGEN / BERLIN / MADRID / TOKYO

Published by
Amsco Publications
257 Park Avenue South, New York, NY 10010 USA

Exclusive Distributors for the United States, Canada, and U.S. possessions:
Hal Leonard Corporation
7777 West Bluemound Road, Milwaukee, WI 53213 USA
Exclusive Distributors for the rest of the world:
Music Sales Limited
Distribution Centre, Newmarket Road, Bury St Edmunds, Suffolk IP33 3YB, UK
Music Sales Pty Limited
20 Resolution Drive, Caringbah, NSW 2229, Australia

Order No. AM999328
ISBN: 978-0-8256-3731-5
HL Item Number: 14037459

Edited by Fiona Bolton

CD mixed and mastered by Jonas Persson

Piano tracks:
Audio recorded and produced by Camden Music
Piano performed by Jessica Maryon-Davies

Other backing tracks:
Audio recorded by Jonas Persson
Backing tracks arranged by Paul Honey
Keyboards by Paul Honey
Guitars by Arthur Dick
Bass by Don Richardson
Drums by Chris Baron

Book illustrations and layout by Liz Barrand

Images courtesy of:
Robin Bradshaw aka Bullit Photography
www.bullitphotography.co.uk
pages 12, 14, 5, 30, 31, 32, 33, 60, 61, 62, 62
63, 91, 92, 93, 102, 103, 104, 105, 158, 159, 223, 224, 225, 226 & 284

English Rose
www.englishroseweddings.co.uk
pages 13, 184, 185, 227, 244, 245, 246 & 247

NOT FOR SALE IN FRANCE, SPAIN, ITALY OR MEXICO

Printed in the United States of America by
Vicks Lithograph and Printing Corporation.

This book celebrates the wedding of

....

to

....

on

....

at

....

....

Introduction

The music used at your wedding is one of the most important aspects of the day. From the processional to the first dance, your choice of songs, pieces and hymns, and the manner of their delivery will have a profound impact on the atmosphere at both the ceremony and reception.

The biggest decision you will make in the planning of your wedding day is whether you want a church service or a civil ceremony. Civil ceremonies cater not only for couples who do not want a Christian service, but also for those who wish to wed in an innovative setting. A church service will include Bible readings and hymns, possibly alongside secular choices, while music and readings used in a civil ceremony must be non-religious and approved by the registrar in advance. Despite these distinctions, it is possible for both types of wedding to carry either a traditional guise or a contemporary twist depending on the choice, not only of décor and dresses, but also of music and readings.

There are a number of options available to you with regards to musical style (classical, pop, jazz or gospel etc.) and manner of performance (pre-recorded or live, instrumentalists or vocalists, soloists or ensembles). Using an organist is an obvious choice, however many modern wedding venues (including some churches) will have a piano instead of an organ, while others may not have either. In these situations using a small ensemble such as a string quartet, wind ensemble or a cappella gospel choir could be a great choice. Your choice may well be impacted by your budget as professional musicians can be expensive. Not for this reason alone, it is worth considering whether you have relatives or friends who are talented musically and who would relish the opportunity to be involved in your special day; this would certainly add a very personal touch. Whatever you choose, try to keep things as simple as possible by using just one or two musicians or ensembles for the entire service. This will keep logistical complications to a minimum, both in advance of your wedding and on the day itself.

The Complete Wedding Music Planner aims to guide you through these and the many other decisions you will make with regards to the music and readings for your wedding. Sheet music in piano solo and piano/vocal arrangements are included for your musicians to use whether friends or professionals. Backing tracks are also included for this purpose, as are demonstrations of the instrumental pieces and piano accompaniments for the hymns.

Usage of the pieces included in this book should not be limited to the section in which they are featured. While they have been placed in the chapter most appropriate to their style or genre, it is far more important that you are happy and comfortable with the service than that it conforms to any standard or tradition. Most of the works contained in the *Processional* and *Recessional* chapters are interchangeable. Similarly, music chosen for the signing of the register could come from almost any chapter. Of greatest importance is that musical elements are selected with the overall service in mind and consideration given to how they relate to the readings and vows.

Order Of Service

Order Of Service

If you have chosen to wed in an Anglican church you will have the choice between a traditional language service (using *The 1662 Book Of Common Prayer*) and a modern language service (using *Common Worship: Services and Prayers for the Church of England*). In either case the option will exist to include communion as part of the service should you wish to. A wedding conducted in a Roman Catholic church will afford you the option of including a full Mass which, if chosen, is usually conducted after the signing of the register.

In all cases the structure of a church ceremony will follow this basic pattern:

Processional

Welcome

Prayer

Hymn

Declarations

Prayer

Readings

Sermon

Hymn

The Marriage
including exchange of vows and rings

Proclamation

Blessing

Signing Of Register

Prayers

Hymn

Dismissal

Recessional

Civil ceremonies tend to be shorter than church services owing to the omission of hymns and prayers, however the structure is very similar:

Processional

Introduction
including declarations

Reading

The Marriage
including exchange of vows and rings

Reading

Signing Of Register

Reading

Recessional

The service could also be elongated by the inclusion of additional secular musical items.

Your order of service will detail the ceremony, including the titles of musical items and readings; and the names of the performers and readers. It may also include the words of any hymns which are to be sung by the congregation, note however that copyright clearance may be required for this.

Examples of orders of service are given on the following pages, and further guidance with regards to the selection of texts—readings, poems and vows—given later in the book.

Entrance Of The Bride

Prelude To Te Deum - Charpentier

Hymn

All Things Bright And Beautiful

Reading

1 Corinthians 13 - Love
Read by Peter Moore

Reading

No. 43 from Sonnets From The Portuguese - Elizabeth Barrett Browning
Read by Mary Crabtree

Hymn

Love Divine, All Loves Excelling

The Marriage

Rev. John Thompson

Prayers

Anna Moore

Signing Of The Register

From This Moment
Sung by Ella Moore

Hymn

Praise My Soul, The King Of Heaven

The Blessing

Exit Of The Bridal Party

Wedding March (from "A Midsummer Night's Dream") - Mendelssohn

Entrance Of The Bride

Everybody's Free
Sung by Bedford Community Gospel Choir

Reading

The Passionate Shepherd To His Love - Christopher Marlowe
Read by James Harris

The Marriage

Reading

These I Can Promise - Mark Twain
Read by Mark Light

Signing Of The Register

Up Where We Belong
Sung by Bedford Community Gospel Choir

Reading

Extract from A Native American Wedding Ceremony
Read by Amy Light

Exit Of The Bridal Party

All You Need Is Love
Sung by Michael Taylor & Bedford Community Gospel Choir

Prelude

Prelude

The music played as your guests arrive will set the tone for the whole day. Aim to provide music for 30 minutes prior to the ceremony, although you, or any live performers, should have more material than required to fill this time slot in order to accommodate any delays in proceedings, not least the late arrival of the bride!

Remember this is only background music—guests will no doubt be chatting among themselves as they eagerly await the arrival of the bridal party—so any performers should not expect attention or applause. That said, the presence of music will create a relaxed and inviting atmosphere, perhaps most appreciated by the groom!

Pre-recorded music is a straight-forward option provided the venue has the facilities for this. If the service is taking place in a church, the organist may be willing to play. Other popular choices are to use a solo piano, string quartet or small wind ensemble.

If hiring a group, ask them for a list of their repertoire and highlight any pieces you particularly like or those by composers with whose other works you are familiar. They should welcome your input and may even be able to accommodate any special requests you have which are not currently in their repertoire.

Your choices need not be limited to classical music. If you have a favorite album by a pop, rock or jazz artist, why not play that? Another nice idea is to make a "mix tape" or playlist of songs that are special to the both of you. Remember though that the bride will not be present at this stage, so ensure any particularly significant songs are retained to be used at another point in the day, such as the first dance.

The following four arragements of classical music are favorites among audiences both familiar and unfamiliar with classical music. They can be played on the piano (as featured on the enclosed CD) or organ, or by an ensemble such as a string quartet or wind quintet. Use these pieces as starting points and find more pieces by your favorite composer, be it Handel or Mozart. There are others elsewhere in this book.

Air from "The Water Music" - Handel 19
Ave Verum Corpus, K618 - Mozart 22
Minuet from "String Quartet" - Boccherini 24
Sheep May Safely Graze - Bach 27

Other suggestions:

Air On The G String - Bach
Canon in D - Pachelbel
Morning from "Peer Gynt Suite" - Grieg
Pavane - Fauré

Air

from "The Water Music"

Composed by George Frideric Handel

Ave Verum Corpus

K618

Composed by Wolfgang Amadeus Mozart

Minuet

from "String Quartet"

Composed by Luigi Boccherini

D.C. al Fine

Sheep May Safely Graze

Composed by Johann Sebastian Bach

Andante moderato

To Coda ⊕

D.C. al Coda

⊕ Coda

rall.

f

p

29

Processional

Processional

The entry of the bride into the wedding venue is a moment of great impact. As such, choosing the right music for this element of the service is of paramount importance. To help you make this decision, ask yourself a few questions: Do you want a fanfare to accompany a glorious procession, or would you prefer a more solemn and stately piece of music? Or perhaps something beautiful and reflective would be in keeping with the style of dress and flowers you have selected?

The processional music should begin just before the bride enters the church or room, and should last until each member of the bridal party has reached their final position. The length of time this takes will obviously depend on the length of the aisle, and as such it is worth timing the procession beforehand. If you want to use a particular piece of music that is significantly longer than the time it will take for the procession, start the music before the bride enters the venue such that the bridal party wait outside rather than at the end of the aisle. If the piece is too short, consider whether or not it can be repeated.

Be aware of the tempo of the piece you chose and whether or not you will be able to walk in sync with the pulse of the music. It does not matter either way but do practice walking to the music beforehand in the shoes you will be wearing on the day!

Again, an organ, piano or instrumental ensemble such as a string quartet is the usual choice of instrumentation to provide the processional music, but there is no reason why a vocal soloist or ensemble could not be used, as in the wedding of Romeo to Juliet in Baz Luhrman's 1996 film in which "Everybody's Free" is used. Another piece used on-screen and included in this book is "Wedding Processional" from *The Sound Of Music;* using this would add a contemporary twist while retaining a traditional feel. A solo or accompanied trumpet is another great idea for this point in the ceremony and would announce the arrival of the bride with great splendor.

If none of the classical pieces featured in this section are what you are looking for, consider one of the pieces of popular music highlighted in the *Signing Of Register* or *First Dance* chapters of this book.

Everybody's Free (To Feel Good)

Words & Music by Tim Cox & Nigel Swanston

Serene

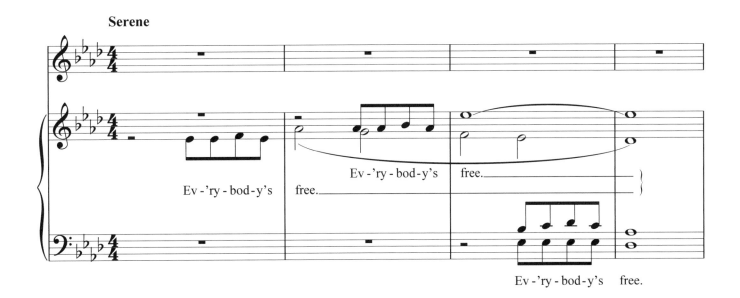

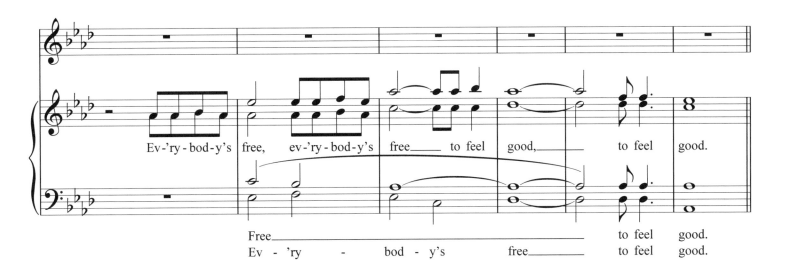

Some - day_ our spi - rit_ will take you_ and guide you there._____ I

Ooh._____

Ooh._____

know you've been hurt - ing_ but I've been wait - ing_ to be there for_ you, and I'll

Ooh._____

Ooh._____

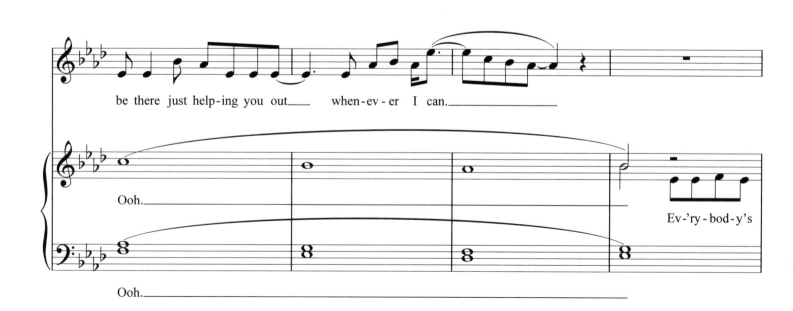

be there just help - ing you out___ when - ev - er I can._____

Ooh._____

Ev - 'ry - bod - y's

Ooh._____

Bridal Chorus

from "Lohengrin"

Composed by Richard Wagner

Con moto moderato

Gloria

from "Gloria"

Composed by Antonio Vivaldi

Allegro

senza rall.

Hornpipe
from "Water Music"

Composed by George Frideric Handel

Prelude To Te Deum

Composed by Marc-Antoine Charpentier

Trumpet Tune

Composed by Henry Purcell

Allegro maestoso

Trumpet Voluntary

Composed by Jeremiah Clarke

rall. al fine

Ped.   *

Wedding Processional

Composed by Richard Rodgers

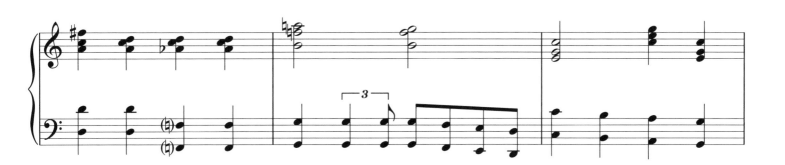

For the entrance of the Bride

rit.

a tempo

Hymns

Hymns

*T*wo or three hymns, either traditional or contemporary, are usually sung by the congregation as part of a church wedding. If you attend church on a regular basis you may well have hymns that are special to you. If not, you may have a favorite from your school days.

In either case, consider whether or not the majority of your guests are likely to be familiar with your choices. If weddings (and funerals) are the only time that most of your friends enter a church, choosing modern worship songs will probably result in somewhat lacklustre singing. A wiser decision would be to chose traditional hymns that are universally well-known.

If you are getting married at Christmas or Easter-time, or on another occasion of religious significance, consider including a Christmas carol, Easter hymn or another song appropriate to the time of year.

Hymns are most often accompanied by a piano or organ and you should discuss your choice with the musician in advance, whether or not they are associated with the church, to ensure they are familiar with those you have selected as well as to discuss your preferred tempo (speed) and how many verses you wish to be sung.

In modern churches contemporary worship songs may be accompanied by a small backing band comprising keyboards, rhythm guitar, bass guitar and drums, and led by a vocalist. If using amplified instruments, talk to the minister of the church with regards to the provisions made for this and whether or not it will be suitable in terms of acoustics.

If you are using a string or wind ensemble in other parts of the service, they may be able to accompany the hymns if the congregation is not too large (and therefore loud). Similarly, if using a vocal ensemble such as a gospel choir, it may be appropriate for them to take a focal point in leading the congregational singing, although accompaniment of some kind will probably still be required.

The words of the hymns are often printed as part of the order of service, however you should note the comment regarding copyright law on page nine. Alternatively the church may have hymns books; if using these, check the number of verses printed beforehand and select from these if there are several.

Religious music is not permitted as part of civil ceremonies, and as such extra readings usually take the place of hymns. However, if you wish to include some congregational singing you could pick a non-religious classic such as "Lean On Me" by Bill Withers.

All Things Bright And Beautiful 67
Amazing Grace 70
Dear Lord And Father Of Mankind 73
Guide Me, O Thou Great Redeemer 76
Jerusalem 78
Lord Of All Hopefullness 82
Love Divine, All Loves Excelling 85
Praise, My Soul, The King Of Heaven 88

Other suggestions:

Joyful, Joyful
Make Me A Channel Of Your Peace
Morning Has Broken
My Jesus, My Savior
Shine, Jesus Shine

All Things Bright And Beautiful

Traditional Melody
Arranged by Martin Shaw
Words by Cecil F. Alexander

D.C. al Coda   ⊕ *Coda*

Verse 2:
The purple-headed mountain,
The river running by,
The sunset and the morning
That brightens up the sky.
(Refrain)

Verse 3:
The cold wind in the winter,
The pleasant summer sun,
The ripe fruits in the garden,
He made them every one.
(Refrain)

Verse 4:
He gave us eyes to see them,
And lips that we might tell
How great is God Almighty,
Who has made all things well.
(Refrain)

Amazing Grace

Words & Music by John Newton

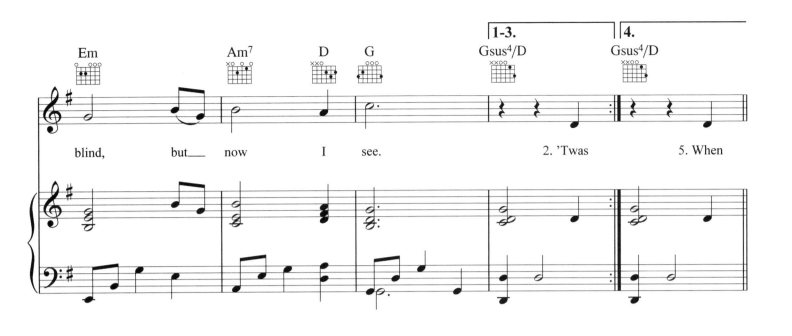

blind, but___ now I see. 2. 'Twas 5. When

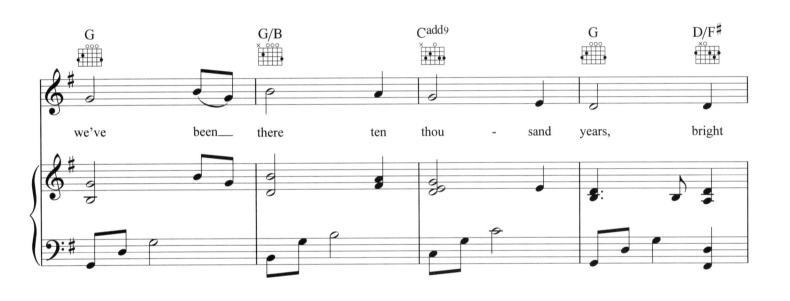

we've been___ there ten thou - sand years, bright

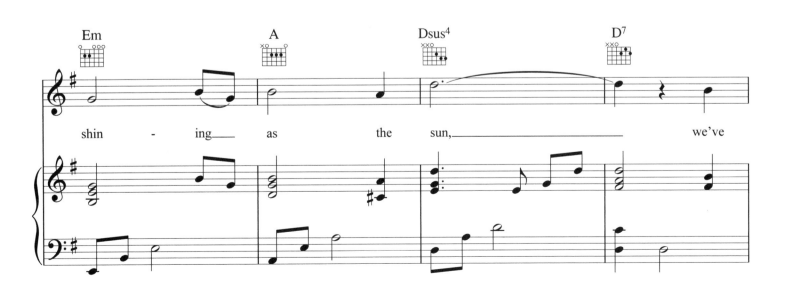

shin - ing___ as the sun,_____ we've

no_____ less___ days to sing_____ God's_ praise than

when we'd__ first be - gun._____

Verse 2:

'Twas grace that taught my heart to fear,
And grace my fears relieved.
How precious did that grace appear
The hour I first believed.

Verse 3:

Through many dangers, toils, and snares
I have already come;
'Tis grace hath brought me safe thus far,
And grace will lead me home.

Verse 4:

The Lord has promised good to me,
His word my hope secures;
He will my shield and portion be
As long as life endures.

Dear Lord And Father Of Mankind

Words by John Greenleaf Whittier
Music by Frederick C. Maker

flesh re - tire; speak through the earth - quake, wind and__ fire, O__

still, small voice of__ calm; O still, small voice of calm.

Verse 3:
O Sabbath rest by Galilee!
O calm of hills above,
Where Jesus knelt to share with Thee
The silence of eternity
Interpreted by love!
Interpreted by love!

Verse 4:
Drop Thy still dews of quietness,
Till all our strivings cease;
Take from our souls the strain and stress,
And let our ordered lives confess
The beauty of Thy peace;
The beauty of Thy peace.

Guide Me, O Thou Great Redeemer

Words by William Williams
Music by John Hughes

Verse 2:

Open now the crystal fountain,
Whence the healing stream doth flow;
Let the fire and cloudy pillar
Lead me all my journey through;
Strong Deliverer, strong Deliverer,
Be Thou still my strength and shield,
Be Thou still my strength and shield.

Verse 3:

When I tread the verge of Jordan,
Bid my anxious fears subside;
Death of death, and Hell's destruction,
Land me safe on Canaan's side;
Songs of praises, songs of praises,
I will ever give to Thee,
I will ever give to Thee.

Jerusalem

Composed by Hubert Parry

Bring me my bow of burn-ing___ gold! Bring me my

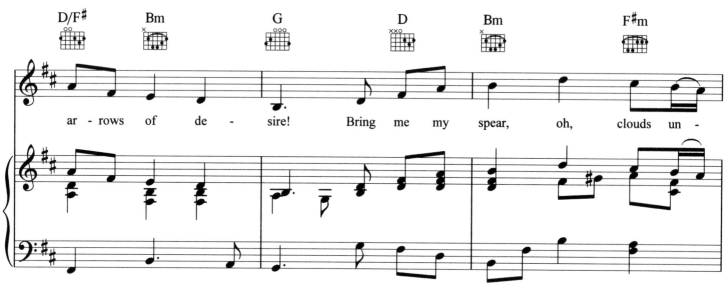

ar-rows of de - sire! Bring me my spear, oh, clouds un -

-fold! Bring me my char-i-ot of fire! I will not

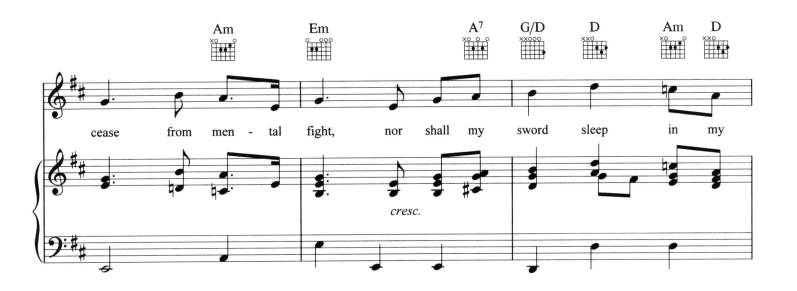

cease from men - tal fight, nor shall my sword sleep in my

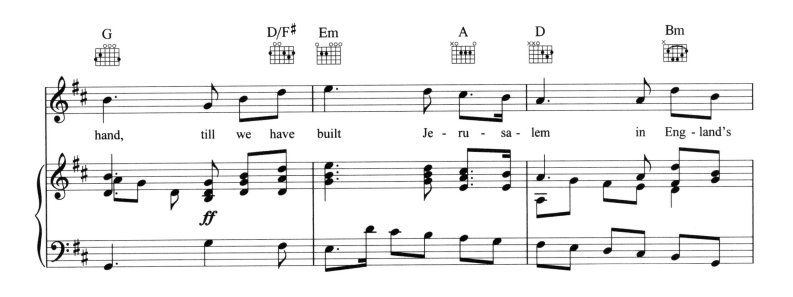

hand, till we have built Je - ru - sa - lem in Eng - land's

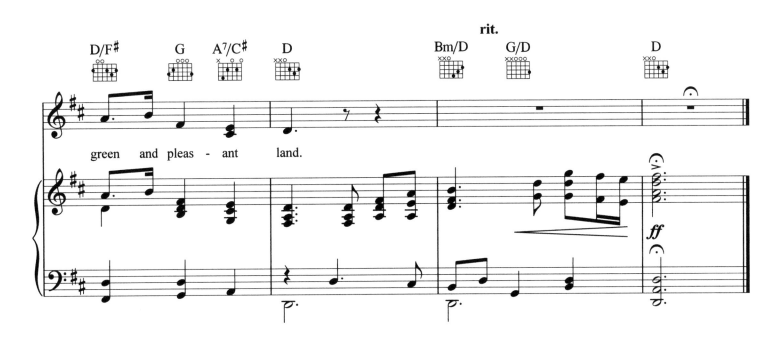

green and pleas - ant land.

Lord Of All Hopefulness

Traditional Melody
Words by Jan Struther (1901-53) from *Enlarged Songs of Praise*, 1931

Moderately, with feeling ♩ = 96

1. Lord of all hope-ful-ness, Lord of all joy, whose
(Verses 2 and 3, see block lyrics)

trust, ev-er child-like, no cares could de-stroy, be

there at our wa-king, and give us, we pray, your

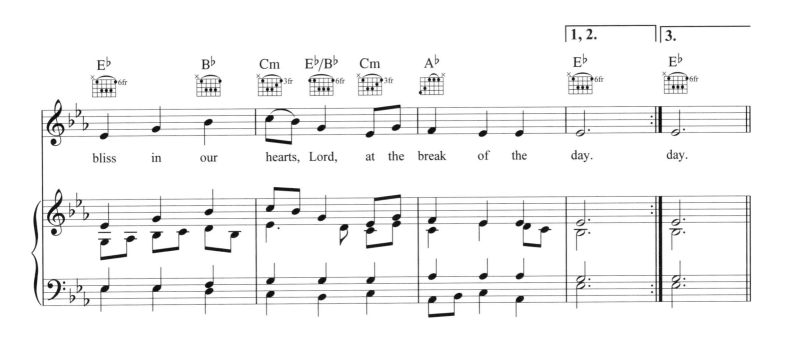

bliss in our hearts, Lord, at the break of the day. day.

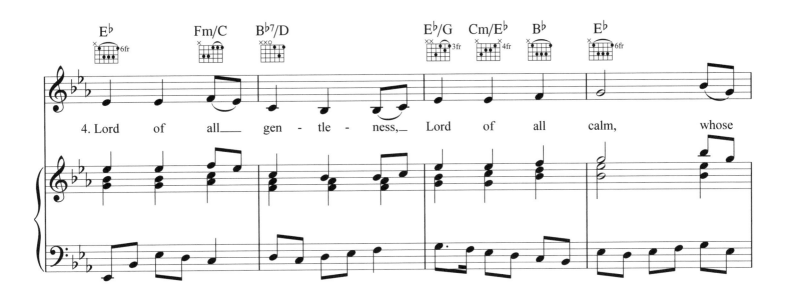

4. Lord of all___ gen - tle - ness,___ Lord of all calm, whose

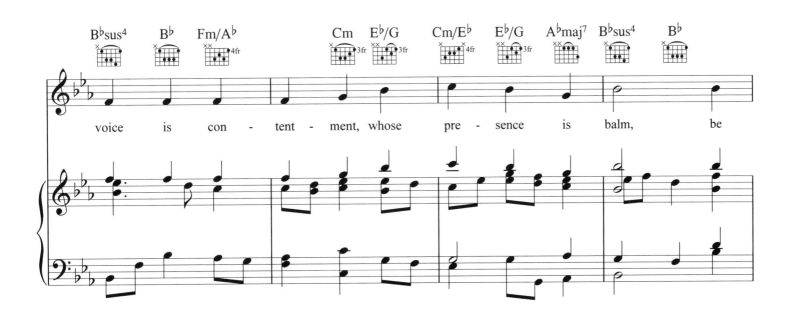

voice is con - tent - ment, whose pre - sence is balm, be

there at___ our___ sleep-ing, and give us, we pray, your

peace in our hearts,_ Lord, at the end of the day.

Verse 2:
Lord of all eagerness,
Lord of all faith,
Whose strong hands were skilled
At the plane and the lathe,
Be there at our labors,
And give us, we pray,
Your strength in our hearts, Lord,
At the noon of the day.

Verse 3:
Lord of all kindliness,
Lord of all grace,
Your hands swift to welcome,
Your arms to embrace,
Be there at our homing,
And give us, we pray,
Yur love in our hearts, Lord,
At the eve of the day.

Love Divine, All Loves Excelling

Words by Charles Wesley
Music by William Rowlands

1. Love div-ine, all
2. Come, al-migh-ty
(Verse 3, see block lyrics)

loves ex-cel-ling, joy of heav'n, to earth come
to de-liv-er, let us all Thy life re-

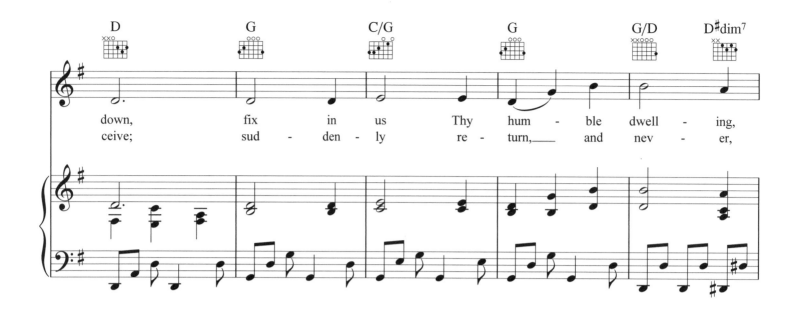

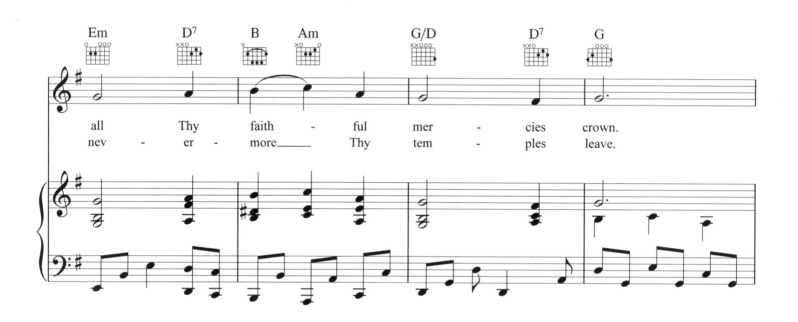

Verse 3:

Finish then Thy new creation;
Pure and spotless let us be;
Let us see Thy great salvation
Perfectly restored in Thee:
Changed from glory into glory,
Till in heaven we take our place,
Till we cast our crowns before Thee,
Lost in wonder, love and praise.

Praise, My Soul, The King Of Heaven

Words by Henry F. Lyte
Music by John Goss

Verse 2:

Praise Him for His grace and favor
To our fathers in distress;
Praise Him still the same for ever,
Slow to chide and swift to bless.
Alleluia, alleluia!
Glorious in His faithfulness.

Verse 3:

Father-like, He tends and spares us;
Well our feeble frame He knows;
In His hand He gently bears us,
Rescues us from all our foes.
Alleluia, alleluia!
Widely yet His mercy flows.

Vows

Vows

$\mathcal{M}$arriage vows are the first legal requirement of the wedding ceremony, the second being the signing of the register. Both church weddings and civil ceremonies must incorporate statutory declaratory and contracting statements, to be said by both the bride and groom, in order for the marriage to be lawful.

The following traditional statements are most often used:

Declaration:

I do solemnly declare that I know not of any lawful impediment why I, N, may not be joined in matrimony to N.

Contraction:

I call upon these persons here present to witness that I, N, do take thee, N, to be my lawful wedded husband/wife.

However, the following variations are also legal:

Declaration:

I declare that I know of no legal reason why I ,N, may not be joined in marriage to N.
or
By replying "I am" to the question, "Are you, N, free lawfully to marry N?"

Contraction:

I,N, take you, N, to be my wedded husband/wife.
or
I, N, take thee, N, to be my wedded husband/wife.

Within a church service additional vows will be specified by either *The 1662 Book of Common Prayer* or *Common Worship: Services and Prayers for the Church of England*, dependant on whether you have chosen a traditional or modern language service. These texts include such phrases as "for richer, for poorer" and concern the exchange of rings. There is very limited scope to vary from these set texts; you may be able to substitute certain words but this will depend on the minister officiating the ceremony.

Declarations

Minister:

N, wilt thou have this woman to thy wedded wife, to live together after God's ordinance in the holy estate of Matrimony?
Wilt thou love her, comfort her, honor, and keep her in sickness and in health;
and, forsaking all other, keep thee only unto her, so long as ye both shall live?

Response:
I will.

Minister:

N, wilt thou have this man to thy wedded husband, to live together after God's ordinance in the holy estate of Matrimony?
Wilt thou obey him, and serve him, love, honor, and keep him in sickness and in health;
and, forsaking all other, keep thee only unto him, so long as ye both shall live?

Response:
I will.

The Marriage

I, N, take thee, N, to be my wedded wife, to have and to hold from this day forward,
for better for worse, for richer for poorer, in sickness and in health, to love and to cherish,
till death us do part, according to God's holy ordinance; and thereto I plight thee my troth.

I, N, take thee, N, to be my wedded husband, to have and to hold from this day forward,
for better for worse, for richer for poorer, in sickness and in health, to love, cherish, and to obey,
till death us do part, according to God's holy ordinance; and thereto I give thee my troth.

The Exchange Of Rings

With this ring I thee wed, with my body I thee worship, and with all my worldly goods I thee endow:
In the Name of the Father, and of the Son, and of the Holy Ghost.
Amen.

Declarations

Minister:
N, will you take N to be your wife?
Will you love her, comfort her, honor and protect her,
and, forsaking all others, be faithful to her as long as you both shall live?

Response:
I will.

Minister:
N, will you take N to be your husband?
Will you love him, comfort him, honor and protect him,
and, forsaking all others, be faithful to him as long as you both shall live?

Response:
I will.

The Marriage

I, N, take you, N, to be my wife, to have and to hold from this day forward;
for better, for worse, for richer, for poorer, in sickness and in health, to love
and to cherish, till death us do part; according to God's holy law.
In the presence of God I make this vow.

I, N, take you, N, to be my husband, to have and to hold from this day forward;
for better, for worse, for richer, for poorer, in sickness and in health, to love and
to cherish, till death us do part; according to God's holy law.
In the presence of God I make this vow.

The Exchange Of Rings

N, I give you this ring as a sign of our marriage. With my body I honor you,
all that I am I give to you, and all that I have I share with you, within the love
of God, Father, Son and Holy Spirit.

A civil ceremony affords you the opportunity to write your own vows, to be said in addition to the statutory statements. This is a beautiful way to personalize the ceremony, however all vows must be approved by the registrar in advance of the ceremony.

Firstly, decide whether you will write your vows together or individually. If you decide to write them independently of each other, agree on a length to ensure one set is not much shorter than the other.

You may find it useful to structure your vows along the same lines as the Anglican vows.

> Declare your intent to marry; that you are free to do so and that you do so willingly.
> Commit to love and care for your partner; to journey together through good times and bad.
> Explain the symbolism of the exchange of rings; an unending symbol of an enduring love.

Think about how you want to start and end your vows, perhaps using one of the following:

> *From this day on, I, N, take you, my beloved N, to be my husband/wife.*
> *I, N, choose you, N, as my best friend, my love for life.*
> *It is an honor that today I, N, take you, N, to be my partner on life's journey.*
> *Today, N, our lives become one.*
>
> *This I pledge to you.*
> *This is my solemn promise to you.*
> *With you will I walk from this day onwards.*
> *For the rest of my life.*

Reminisce on how you met; particular events or special moments you have shared; holidays, journeys, birthdays, concerts. Consider your hopes and dreams for your life together.

Sincerity—Honesty is imperative in writing your own vows. The words you say must come from your heart. If you struggle to express yourself, why not use a poem or a set of song lyrics?

Humor—Feel free to temper your vows with a light-hearted sentiment but do not make a joke of what is a very serious commitment.

Rehearse your vows as you would do any presentation or speech, committing them to memory if you are able. However, ensure you have a copy of your vows handy on your wedding day to avoid worrying about whether or not you will remember them. As with the vows of the Anglican church, you could repeat your vows after the celebrant.

On the next page are key words to aid and inspire you in writing your vows. On the following page are some example vows which you could tailor to make your own.

Chose, Desire,

Honor, Privilege,

Welcome, Freely

Beloved, Best friend, Confidant, Partner for life

Promise, Pledge

Emotional, Spiritual

Heart, Hand, Body, Mind, Soul

Devotion, Commitment, Loyalty

Forever, Constant, Unconditional, Faithful, Trustworthy

Live, Love, Support, Respect, Honor, Shelter, Care,

Comfort, Share, Serve, Obey, Provide for, Hold, Guide,

Listen, Laugh, Cry, Play

Joy, Love, Patience, Hope, Fulfillment, Strength, Belonging

Sacrifice, Compromise, Struggle

Solace, Hardships, Trouble

Dreams, Fears, Goals, Worries, Desires

Two flames, one light

Hand in hand, heart in heart

Stand by your side

Never walk alone

Today, I, N, chose you, N, as my husband/wife.
I promise you my deepest love and my fullest devotion
whatever the future may hold for us.
I promise to be faithful to you;
To laugh with you in times of joy,
To comfort you in times of sorrow;
To delight in you in times of success,
To lend you strength in times of trouble;
To cherish our friendship in times of bliss,
To be your shelter in times of strife.
From this day forward, I shall love you.
This is my promise to you.

N, I give you my body, my mind, my heart, and my soul.
Everything that I have, now belongs to you.
I will follow you anywhere and everywhere you lead,
through the pressures of the present and the uncertainties of the future.
You shall not walk alone.

Today, I join my life to yours.
My love shall reside in your heart,
And yours in mine.
I will bring out the best in you,
As you bring out the best in me.
If you need rest, lean upon my shoulder.
If you need shelter, find comfort in my arms.
Take my hand and walk with me, until our lives end.

I, N, take you, not only as my husband/wife, but as my friend,
my lover, my confidant, my companion for life.
I give you this ring as a sign of my commitment to our love,
and the life we will share together.
Come what may, this shall remain my promise to you.

Signing Of Register

Signing Of Register

The signing of the register is an opportunity for you to pick almost any piece of music. Classical or pop, instrumental or vocal, your selection of repertoire for this part of the ceremony could be vintage or modern, and could be performed by a soloist or ensemble.

It also presents the perfect opportunity to involve a close friend or member of your family who has not already been given a role as a bridesmaid or an usher, and who has either an instrumental or vocal talent.

The works featured in this chapter, with the exception of the instrumental piece by Satie, are for voice and piano. They draw on universally favorite classical repertoire as well as songs from the sphere of popular music with eminently suitable lyrics regarding love and relationships.

Most of the songs would also work well with the melody line played on an instrument such as the flute, saxophone or violin. They could also be accompanied on guitar or performed using the backing tracks on the enclosed CD.

A number of the pieces included here draw inspiration from on-screen weddings: Paul McCartney's "My Love" was performed by a string quartet at the wedding of Monica to Chandler in *Friends*; and Angry Anderson provided the soundtrack to everyone's favorite Australian soap wedding, that of Scott and Charlene in *Neighbours*, with "Suddenly."

Others have been used as love themes in films although not as part of weddings, namely "Come What May" from *Moulin Rouge* and "Up Where We Belong" from *An Officer & A Gentleman.*

Other suggestions:

Endless Love – Diana Ross & Lionel Ritchie

Gabriel's Oboe from *The Mission* – Ennio Morricone

Lean On Me – Bill Withers

The Rose from *The Rose* – Bette Midler, also performed by LeAnn Rimes and Westlife

Stand By Me – Ben E. King

Truly, Madly, Deeply – Savage Garden

Your Song – Elton John

Gymnopédie No. 1

Composed by Erik Satie

Lent et douloureux

Ave Maria

Composed by Franz Schubert

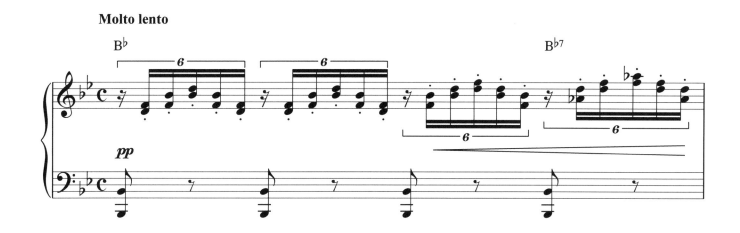

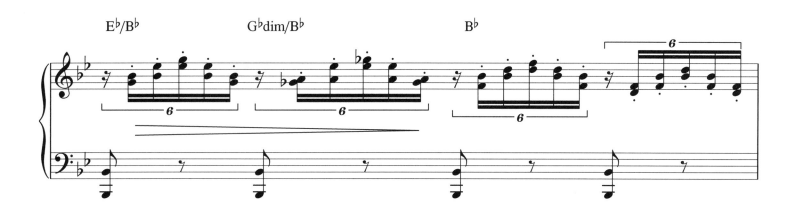

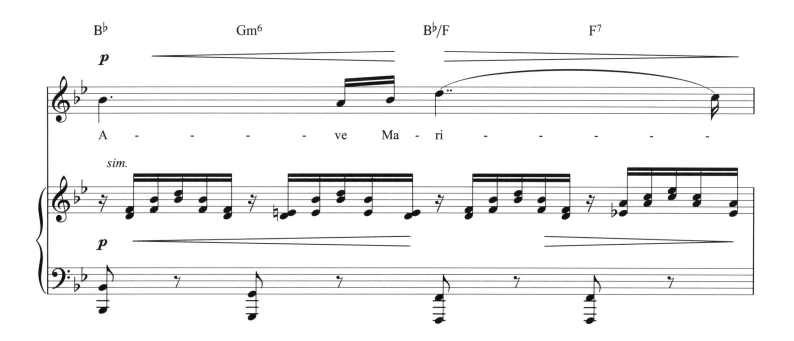

pien' di spe - me si pro - stra ai tuoi piè, t'in -

-vo - ca e atten - de che tu de - di - a la

pa - ce che so - lo tu puoi do - nar.

116

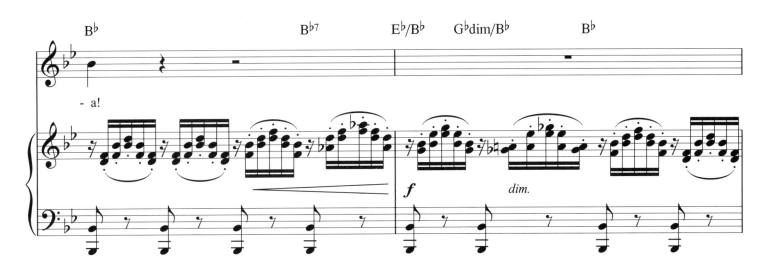

Panis Angelicus

Composed by César Franck

Pau - per, pau - per, ser - vus et hu - mi - lis.

Pa - nis an - ge - li - cus fit pa - nis ho - mi - num.

Dat panis coe - li - cus fi - gu - ris ter - mi - num.

O res mi - ra - bi - lis man - du - cat Do - mi - num.

Pau - per,— pau - per, ser - vus et hu - mi - lis.

Pau - per,— pau - per, ser - vus,— ser - vus et hu - mi -

- lis.

Come What May

Words & Music by David Baerwald

rit.

I will love you. Sud-den-ly the world seems such a per-fect place.

you.

a tempo

Come what may. Come what may.

Come what may. Come what may.

I will love you un-til my dy-ing day.

I will love you un-til my dy-ing day.

127

From This Moment On

Words & Music by Shania Twain and R. J. Lange

prom - ise you this.___ There is noth - ing I would - n't give,___ from this mo - ment. I will love___ you___ as long as I live,___ from this mo - ment___ on. Mm___ mm___ mm.

I Swear

Words & Music by Gary Baker & Frank Myers

My Love

Words & Music by Paul and Linda McCartney

142

Suddenly

Words & Music by Gary Anderson,
Andrew Cichon & Kevin Beamish

Sud - den - ly____ o - pen - ly,____ you're

146

Up Where We Belong

Words by Will Jennings
Music by Buffy Sainte-Marie and Jack Nitzsche

You Take My Breath Away

Words & Music by Claire Hamill

E   Esus⁴   E   Esus⁴   E

___ a - way.

1. You watch my love grow
2. Your beau - ty is there in

Instrumental till *

Esus⁴/2   E   Esus⁴/2

like a___ child,   some-times_ gen - tle and some - times_ wild;___
all I see___   and when I feel your eyes on me,___ oh,

Asus²   B   E   Esus⁴

some - times___ you just___ take my ___ breath_ a - way.
don't you know,___ you just___ take my ___ breath a - way.___

E   Bsus⁴   B   E

* And it's too good to slip by, too___ good to lose.___

Oh,___ yes, you take_____ my_ breath a - way._____

Readings

Readings

*J*ust as the choices you make in respect of the music for your wedding will shape and color the day, the readings you select will convey a message to your guests about yourselves, your relationship and your hopes for the future.

Readings can include passages from the Bible, poems and prose. They may be traditional or modern, and can be serious or light-hearted. You could use a quote from a play or film (such as "The Apache Wedding Prayer," written for the 1950 western film *Broken Arrow*), or an extract from a favorite book (such as *Captain Corelli's Mandolin* by Louis de Bernières). You could select a reading from another culture such as a Chinese poem, a comical reading along the lines of "A Good Wedding Cake," or an extract from a children's book such as Sam McBratney's *Guess How Much I Love You* or *The Complete Poems of Winnie-the-Pooh* by A. A. Milne.

Readings also afford the perfect opportunity to involve family and friends, however you should ensure that they are well-rehearsed and that the selected texts are of an appropriate length.

Texts used in civil ceremonies should have no religious content (Christian or otherwise) and as such you should seek approval of your choices from the registrar in advance of the ceremony.

Contained in this chapter are a variety of texts suitable for both church services and civil ceremonies. Of course, there are plenty of others to chose from.

Other suggestions:

A Subaltern's Love Song by John Betjeman
Tell Me The Truth About Love by W. H. Auden
The Divine Comedy by Dante
Romeo and Juliet by William Shakespeare

In the case of church services, at least one reading will be taken from the Bible.

There are several different translations of the Bible, ranging from traditional such as the King James Version, to modern paraphrases such as *The Message*. This alone can have a significant impact on an extract. For example, the King James Version of 1 Corinthians 13, well-known as "The Love Chapter," does not use the word "love," instead it speaks of "charity."

⁴Charity suffereth long, and is kind; charity envieth not; charity vaunteth not itself, is not puffed up.
⁵Doth not behave itself unseemly, seeketh not her own, is not easily provoked, thinketh no evil.
(King James Version)

⁴Love is patient, love is kind. It does not envy, it does not boast, it is not proud.
⁵It is not rude, it is not self-seeking, it is not easily angered, it keeps no record of wrongs.
(New International Version)

Love never gives up.
Love cares more for others than for self.
Love doesn't want what it doesn't have.
Love doesn't strut,
Doesn't have a swelled head,
Doesn't force itself on others,
Isn't always "me first,"
Doesn't fly off the handle,
Doesn't keep score of the sins of others,
(The Message)

Consider which of these styles you prefer and which is in keeping with the other choices you have made. It is important to discuss your choice of translation with the minister of the church in which you are to be married, as they may have particular regulations.

The Bible is a big book and selecting a passage from it may seem a daunting task. Contained in this chapter are a number of readings taken from both the old and new testaments; if including two Bible readings in your ceremony it is a nice idea to use one from each. Some extracts concern the topic of love, either between man and woman, or brotherly Christian love. Alternatively you could select a Psalm of praise and worship, or a Proverb on the topic of marriage. Perhaps you have a favorite Bible verse or one that you remember from school or Sunday school? Within reason, it does not need to link into the ideas of love and marriage. Indeed, it is likely that the minister will share a short thought or sermon within the ceremony and may be able to link your selected passage to this.

Extract from

Arcadia

Sir Philip Sydney (1554-1586)

My true-love hath my heart and I have his,

By just exchange one for the other given:

I hold his dear, and mine he cannot miss;

There never was a bargain better driven.

His heart in me keeps me and him in one;

My heart in him, his thoughts and senses guides:

He loves my heart, for once it was his own;

I cherish his because in me it bides.

His heart his wound received from my sight;

My heart was wounded with his wounded heart;

For as from me on him his hurt did light,

So still, methought, in me his hurt did smart:

Both equal hurt, in this change sought our bliss,

My true love hath my heart and I have his.

Extract from

De Imitatio Christi

Thomas à Kempis (1379-1471)

Love is an excellent thing, a very great blessing, indeed. It makes every difficulty easy, and bears all wrongs with equanimity. For it bears a burden without being weighted and renders sweet all that is bitter. The noble love of Jesus spurs to great deeds and excites longing for that which is more perfect. Love tends upward; it will not be held down by anything low. Love wishes to be free and estranged from all worldly affections, lest its inward sight be obstructed, lest it be entangled in any temporal interest and overcome by adversity.

Nothing is sweeter than love, nothing stronger or higher or wider; nothing is more pleasant, nothing fuller, and nothing better in heaven or on earth, for love is born of God and cannot rest except in God, Who is above all created things.

One who is in love flies, runs, and rejoices; he is free, not bound. He gives all for all and possesses all in all, because he rests in the one sovereign Good, Who is above all things, and from Whom every good flows and proceeds. He does not look to the gift but turns himself above all gifts to the Giver.

Love often knows no limits but overflows all bounds. Love feels no burden, thinks nothing of troubles, attempts more than it is able, and does not plead impossibility, because it believes that it may and can do all things. For this reason, it is able to do all, performing and effecting much where he who does not love fails and falls.

Love is watchful. Sleeping, it does not slumber. Wearied, it is not tired. Pressed, it is not straitened. Alarmed, it is not confused, but like a living flame, a burning torch, it forces its way upward and passes unharmed through every obstacle.

No. 43

from Sonnets from the Portuguese

Elizabeth Barrett Browning (1806-1861)

How do I love thee? Let me count the ways.

I love thee to the depth and breadth and height

My soul can reach, when feeling out of sight

For the ends of Being and ideal Grace.

I love thee to the level of everyday's

Most quiet need, by sun and candlelight.

I love thee freely, as men strive for Right;

I love thee purely, as they turn from Praise.

I love thee with the passion put to use

In my old griefs, and with my childhood's faith.

I love thee with a love I seemed to lose

With my lost saints,—I love thee with the breath,

Smiles, tears, of all my life!—and, if God choose,

I shall but love thee better after death.

Extract from

Les Misérables

Victor Hugo (1802-1885)

You can give without loving, but you can never love without giving.

The great acts of love are done by those who are habitually performing small

acts of kindness. We pardon to the extent that we love.

Love is knowing that even when you are alone, you will never be lonely again.

And great happiness of life is the conviction that we are loved.

Loved for ourselves. And even loved in spite of ourselves.

Extract from

A Native American Wedding Ceremony

Author unknown

May the sun bring you new happiness by day;

May the moon softly restore you by night;

May the rain wash away your worries

And the breeze blow new strength into your being,

And all the days of your life

May you walk gently through the world

and know its beauty.

Extract from

Love Lives

John Clare (1793-1864)

Love lives beyond

The tomb, the earth, which fades like dew.

I love the fond,

The faithful, and the true.

Love lies in sleep,

The happiness of healthy dreams,

Eve's dews may weep,

But love delightful seems.

'Tis seen in flowers,

And in the even's pearly dew

On earth's green hours,

And in the heaven's eternal blue.

'Tis heard in spring

When light and sunbeams, warm and kind,

On angel's wing

Bring love and music to the wind.

And where is voice

So young, so beautiful, so sweet

As nature's choice,

Where spring and lovers meet?

Love lies beyond

The tomb, the earth, the flowers, and dew.

I love the fond,

The faithful, young, and true.

Marriage

from The Prophet

Kahlil Gibran (1883-1931)

Then Almitra spoke again and said, "And what of Marriage, master?"

And he answered saying:

You were born together, and together you shall be forevermore.

You shall be together when white wings of death scatter your days.

Aye, you shall be together even in the silent memory of God.

But let there be spaces in your togetherness,

And let the winds of the heavens dance between you.

Love one another but make not a bond of love:

Let it rather be a moving sea between the shores of your souls.

Fill each other's cup but drink not from one cup.

Give one another of your bread but eat not from the same loaf.

Sing and dance together and be joyous, but let each one of you be alone,

Even as the strings of a lute are alone though they quiver with the same music.

Give your hearts, but not into each other's keeping.

For only the hand of Life can contain your hearts.

And stand together, yet not too near together:

For the pillars of the temple stand apart,

And the oak tree and the cypress grow not in each other's shadow.

Then said Almitra, "Speak to us of Love."

And he raised his head and looked upon the people, and there fell a stillness upon them.

And with a great voice he said:

When love beckons to you follow him,

Though his ways are hard and steep.

And when his wings enfold you yield to him,

Though the sword hidden among his pinions may wound you.

And when he speaks to you believe in him,

Though his voice may shatter your dreams as the north wind lays waste the garden.

For even as love crowns you so shall he crucify you.

The Passionate Shepherd
To His Love

Christopher Marlowe (1564-1593)

Come live with me and be my love,
And we will all the pleasures prove
That valleys, groves, hills, and fields,
Woods, or steepy mountain yields.

And we will sit upon the rocks,
Seeing the shepherds feed their flocks,
By shallow rivers to whose falls
Melodious birds sing madrigals.

And I will make thee beds of roses
And a thousand fragrant posies,
A cap of flowers, and a kirtle
Embroidered all with leaves of myrtle;

A gown made of the finest wool
Which from our pretty lambs we pull;
Fair lined slippers for the cold,
With buckles of the purest gold;

A belt of straw and ivy buds,
With coral clasps and amber studs:
And if these pleasures may thee move,
Come live with me, and be my love.

The shepherds' swains shall dance and sing
For thy delight each May morning:
If these delights thy mind may move,
Then live with me and be my love.

Never Marry But For Love

William Penn (1644-1718)

Never marry but for love; but see that thou lovest what is lovely. He that minds a body and not a soul has not the better part of that relationship, and will consequently lack the noblest comfort of a married life.

Between a man and his wife nothing ought rule but love. As love ought to bring them together, so it is the best way to keep them well together.

A husband and wife that love one another show their children that they should do so too. Others visibly lose their authority in their families by their contempt of one another, and teach their children to be unnatural by their own examples.

Let not enjoyment lessen, but augment, affection; it being the basest of passions to like when we have not, what we slight when we possess.

Here it is we ought to search out our pleasure, where the field is large and full of variety, and of an enduring nature; sickness, poverty or disgrace being not able to shake it because it is not under the moving influences of worldly contingencies.

Nothing can be more entire and without reserve; nothing more zealous, affectionate and sincere; nothing more contented than such a couple, nor greater temporal felicity than to be one of them.

A Red, Red Rose

Robert Burns (1759-1796)

O my Luve's like a red, red rose,
That's newly sprung in June:
O my Luve's like the melodie,
That's sweetly play'd in tune.

As fair art thou, my bonie lass,
So deep in luve am I;
And I will luve thee still, my dear,
Till a' the seas gang dry.

Till a' the seas gang dry, my dear,
And the rocks melt wi' the sun;
And I will luve thee still, my dear,
While the sands o' life shall run.

And fare-thee-weel, my only Luve!
And fare-thee-weel, a while!
And I will come again, my Luve,
Tho' 'twere ten thousand mile!

Sonnet 18

William Shakespeare (1564-1616)

Shall I compare thee to a summer's day?

Thou art more lovely and more temperate:

Rough winds do shake the darling buds of May,

And summer's lease hath all too short a date:

Sometime too hot the eye of heaven shines,

And often is his gold complexion dimm'd,

And every fair from fair sometime declines,

By chance, or nature's changing course untrimm'd:

But thy eternal summer shall not fade,

Nor lose possession of that fair thou ow'st,

Nor shall death brag thou wander'st in his shade,

When in eternal lines to time thou grow'st,

So long as men can breathe, or eyes can see,

So long lives this, and this gives life to thee.

To My Dear and Loving Husband

Anne Bradstreet (1612-1672)

If ever two were one, then surely we.

If ever man were lov'd by wife, then thee.

If ever wife was happy in a man,

Compare with me, ye women, if you can.

I prize thy love more than whole Mines of gold

Or all the riches that the East doth hold.

My love is such that Rivers cannot quench,

Nor ought but love from thee give recompense.

Thy love is such I can no way repay.

The heavens reward thee manifold, I pray.

Then while we live, in love let's so persevere

That when we live no more, we may live ever

These I Can Promise

Mark Twain (1835-1910)

I cannot promise you a life of sunshine;

I cannot promise you riches, wealth or gold;

I cannot promise you an easy pathway

That leads away from change or growing old.

But I can promise all my heart's devotion;

A smile to chase away your tears of sorrow.

A love that's true and ever growing;

A hand to hold in your's through each tomorrow.

Genesis 2

¹⁸ And the LORD God said, It is not good that the man should be alone; I will make him an help meet for him.

¹⁹ And out of the ground the LORD God formed every beast of the field, and every fowl of the air; and brought them unto Adam to see what he would call them: and whatsoever Adam called every living creature, that was the name thereof.

²⁰ And Adam gave names to all cattle, and to the fowl of the air, and to every beast of the field; but for Adam there was not found an help meet for him.

²¹ And the LORD God caused a deep sleep to fall upon Adam, and he slept: and he took one of his ribs, and closed up the flesh instead thereof;

²² And the rib, which the LORD God had taken from man, made he a woman, and brought her unto the man.

²³ And Adam said, This is now bone of my bones, and flesh of my flesh: she shall be called Woman, because she was taken out of Man.

²⁴ Therefore shall a man leave his father and his mother, and shall cleave unto his wife: and they shall be one flesh.

Psalm 95

¹ O come, let us sing unto the LORD:
let us make a joyful noise to the rock of our salvation.
² Let us come before his presence with thanksgiving,
and make a joyful noise unto him with psalms.
³ For the LORD is a great God,
and a great King above all gods.
⁴ In his hand are the deep places of the earth:
the strength of the hills is his also.
⁵ The sea is his, and he made it:
and his hands formed the dry land.
⁶ O come, let us worship and bow down:
let us kneel before the LORD our maker.
⁷ For he is our God;
and we are the people of his pasture,
and the sheep of his hand.

Psalm 100

¹ *Make a joyful noise unto the LORD, all ye lands.*
² *Serve the LORD with gladness:*
come before his presence with singing.
³ *Know ye that the LORD he is God:*
it is he that hath made us, and not we ourselves;
we are his people, and the sheep of his pasture.
⁴ *Enter into his gates with thanksgiving,*
and into his courts with praise:
be thankful unto him, and bless his name.
⁵ *For the LORD is good;*
his mercy is everlasting;
and his truth endureth to all generations.

Psalm 121

¹ *I will lift up mine eyes unto the hills,*
from whence cometh my help.
² *My help cometh from the LORD,*
which made heaven and earth.
³ *He will not suffer thy foot to be moved:*
he that keepeth thee will not slumber.
⁴ *Behold, he that keepeth Israel shall neither slumber nor sleep.*
⁵ *The LORD is thy keeper:*
the LORD is thy shade upon thy right hand.
⁶ *The sun shall not smite thee by day,*
nor the moon by night.
⁷ *The LORD shall preserve thee from all evil:*
he shall preserve thy soul.
⁸ *The LORD shall preserve thy going out and thy coming in*
from this time forth, and even for evermore.

Psalm 136

¹ O give thanks unto the LORD; for he is good:
for his mercy endureth for ever.
² O give thanks unto the God of gods:
for his mercy endureth for ever.
³O give thanks to the Lord of lords:
for his mercy endureth for ever.
⁴ To him who alone doeth great wonders:
for his mercy endureth for ever.
⁵ To him that by wisdom made the heavens:
for his mercy endureth for ever.
⁶ To him that stretched out the earth above the waters:
for his mercy endureth for ever.
⁷ To him that made great lights:
for his mercy endureth for ever:
⁸ The sun to rule by day:
for his mercy endureth for ever:
⁹ The moon and stars to rule by night:
for his mercy endureth for ever.
²⁶ Give thanks unto the God of heaven:
for his mercy endureth for ever.

Psalm 150

¹ Praise ye the LORD. Praise God in his sanctuary:
praise him in the firmament of his power.
² Praise him for his mighty acts:
praise him according to his excellent greatness.
³ Praise him with the sound of the trumpet:
praise him with the psaltery and harp.
⁴ Praise him with the timbrel and dance:
praise him with stringed instruments and organs.
⁵ Praise him upon the loud cymbals:
praise him upon the high sounding cymbals.
⁶ Let every thing that hath breath praise the LORD.
Praise ye the LORD.

Proverbs 31

*¹⁰ Who can find a virtuous woman?
for her price is far above rubies.
¹¹ The heart of her husband doth safely trust in her,
so that he shall have no need of spoil.
¹² She will do him good and not evil all the days of her life.
²⁵ Strength and honor are her clothing;
and she shall rejoice in time to come.
²⁶ She openeth her mouth with wisdom;
and in her tongue is the law of kindness.
²⁷ She looketh well to the ways of her household,
and eateth not the bread of idleness.
²⁸ Her children arise up, and call her blessed;
her husband also, and he praiseth her.
²⁹ Many daughters have done virtuously,
but thou excellest them all.
³⁰ Favor is deceitful, and beauty is vain:
but a woman that feareth the LORD, she shall be praised.
³¹ Give her of the fruit of her hands;
and let her own works praise her in the gates.*

Ecclesiastes 4

*⁹ Two are better than one;
because they have a good reward for their labor.
¹⁰ For if they fall, the one will lift up his fellow:
but woe to him that is alone when he falleth;
for he hath not another to help him up.
¹¹ Again, if two lie together, then they have heat:
but how can one be warm alone?
¹² And if one prevail against him, two shall withstand him;
and a threefold cord is not quickly broken.*

Matthew 22

34 But when the Pharisees had heard that he had put the Sadducees to silence, they were gathered together. 35 Then one of them, which was a lawyer, asked him a question, tempting him, and saying, 36 Master, which is the great commandment in the law? 37 Jesus said unto him, Thou shalt love the Lord thy God with all thy heart, and with all thy soul, and with all thy mind. 38 This is the first and great commandment. 39 And the second is like unto it, Thou shalt love thy neighbor as thyself. 40 On these two commandments hang all the law and the prophets.

1 Corinthians 13

1 Though I speak with the tongues of men and of angels, and have not charity, I am become as sounding brass, or a tinkling cymbal. 2 And though I have the gift of prophecy, and understand all mysteries, and all knowledge; and though I have all faith, so that I could remove mountains, and have not charity, I am nothing. 3 And though I bestow all my goods to feed the poor, and though I give my body to be burned, and have not charity, it profiteth me nothing.

4 Charity suffereth long, and is kind; charity envieth not; charity vaunteth not itself, is not puffed up, 5 Doth not behave itself unseemly, seeketh not her own, is not easily provoked, thinketh no evil; 6 Rejoiceth not in iniquity, but rejoiceth in the truth; 7 Beareth all things, believeth all things, hopeth all things, endureth all things.

8 Charity never faileth: but whether there be prophecies, they shall fail; whether there be tongues, they shall cease; whether there be knowledge, it shall vanish away. 9 For we know in part, and we prophesy in part. 10 But when that which is perfect is come, then that which is in part shall be done away. 11 When I was a child, I spake as a child, I understood as a child, I thought as a child: but when I became a man, I put away childish things. 12 For now we see through a glass, darkly; but then face to face: now I know in part; but then shall I know even as also I am known.

13 And now abideth faith, hope, charity, these three; but the greatest of these is charity.

John 15

¹ I am the true vine, and my Father is the husbandman. ² Every branch in me that beareth not fruit he taketh away: and every branch that beareth fruit, he purgeth it, that it may bring forth more fruit. ³ Now ye are clean through the word which I have spoken unto you.
⁴ Abide in me, and I in you. As the branch cannot bear fruit of itself, except it abide in the vine; no more can ye, except ye abide in me.

⁵ I am the vine, ye are the branches: He that abideth in me, and I in him, the same bringeth forth much fruit: for without me ye can do nothing. ⁶ If a man abide not in me, he is cast forth as a branch, and is withered; and men gather them, and cast them into the fire, and they are burned. ⁷ If ye abide in me, and my words abide in you, ye shall ask what ye will, and it shall be done unto you. ⁸ Herein is my Father glorified, that ye bear much fruit; so shall ye be my disciples.

⁹ As the Father hath loved me, so have I loved you: continue ye in my love. ¹⁰ If ye keep my commandments, ye shall abide in my love; even as I have kept my Father's commandments, and abide in his love. ¹¹ These things have I spoken unto you, that my joy might remain in you, and that your joy might be full. ¹² This is my commandment, That ye love one another, as I have loved you. ¹³ Greater love hath no man than this, that a man lay down his life for his friends. ¹⁴ Ye are my friends, if ye do whatsoever I command you. ¹⁵ Henceforth I call you not servants; for the servant knoweth not what his lord doeth: but I have called you friends; for all things that I have heard of my Father I have made known unto you. ¹⁶ Ye have not chosen me, but I have chosen you, and ordained you, that ye should go and bring forth fruit, and that your fruit should remain: that whatsoever ye shall ask of the Father in my name, he may give it you. ¹⁷ These things I command you, that ye love one another.

Romans 12

⁹ Let love be without dissimulation. Abhor that which is evil; cleave to that which is good. ¹⁰ Be kindly affectioned one to another with brotherly love; in honor preferring one another; ¹¹ Not slothful in business; fervent in spirit; serving the Lord; ¹² Rejoicing in hope; patient in tribulation; continuing instant in prayer; ¹³ Distributing to the necessity of saints; given to hospitality.

¹⁴ Bless them which persecute you: bless, and curse not. ¹⁵ Rejoice with them that do rejoice, and weep with them that weep. ¹⁶ Be of the same mind one toward another. Mind not high things, but condescend to men of low estate. Be not wise in your own conceits.

¹⁷ Recompense to no man evil for evil. Provide things honest in the sight of all men.

¹⁸ If it be possible, as much as lieth in you, live peaceably with all men.

1 John 4

⁷ Beloved, let us love one another: for love is of God; and every one that loveth is born of God, and knoweth God. ⁸ He that loveth not knoweth not God; for God is love. ⁹ In this was manifested the love of God toward us, because that God sent his only begotten Son into the world, that we might live through him. ¹⁰ Herein is love, not that we loved God, but that he loved us, and sent his Son to be the propitiation for our sins. ¹¹ Beloved, if God so loved us, we ought also to love one another. ¹² No man hath seen God at any time. If we love one another, God dwelleth in us, and his love is perfected in us.

Ephesians 3

[14]For this cause I bow my knees unto the Father of our Lord Jesus Christ, [15] Of whom the whole family in heaven and earth is named, [16] That he would grant you, according to the riches of his glory, to be strengthened with might by his Spirit in the inner man; [17] That Christ may dwell in your hearts by faith; that ye, being rooted and grounded in love, [18] May be able to comprehend with all saints what is the breadth, and length, and depth, and height; [19] And to know the love of Christ, which passeth knowledge, that ye might be filled with all the fullness of God.

Ephesians 5

[21]Submitting yourselves one to another in the fear of God.

[22]Wives, submit yourselves unto your own husbands, as unto the Lord. [23]For the husband is the head of the wife, even as Christ is the head of the church: and he is the savior of the body. [24] Therefore as the church is subject unto Christ, so let the wives be to their own husbands in every thing.

[25] Husbands, love your wives, even as Christ also loved the church, and gave himself for it; [26] That he might sanctify and cleanse it with the washing of water by the word, [27] That he might present it to himself a glorious church, not having spot, or wrinkle, or any such thing; but that it should be holy and without blemish. [28] So ought men to love their wives as their own bodies. He that loveth his wife loveth himself. [29] For no man ever yet hated his own flesh; but nourisheth and cherisheth it, even as the Lord the church: [30] For we are members of his body, of his flesh, and of his bones. [31] For this cause shall a man leave his father and mother, and shall be joined unto his wife, and they two shall be one flesh. [32] This is a great mystery: but I speak concerning Christ and the church. [33] Nevertheless let every one of you in particular so love his wife even as himself; and the wife see that she reverence her husband.

Colossians 3

¹ If ye then be risen with Christ, seek those things which are above, where Christ sitteth on the right hand of God. ² Set your affection on things above, not on things on the earth. ³ For ye are dead, and your life is hid with Christ in God. ⁴ When Christ, who is our life, shall appear, then shall ye also appear with him in glory.

⁵ Mortify therefore your members which are upon the earth; fornication, uncleanness, inordinate affection, evil concupiscence, and covetousness, which is idolatry: ⁶ For which things' sake the wrath of God cometh on the children of disobedience: ⁷ In the which ye also walked some time, when ye lived in them. ⁸ But now ye also put off all these; anger, wrath, malice, blasphemy, filthy communication out of your mouth.

⁹ Lie not one to another, seeing that ye have put off the old man with his deeds; ¹⁰ And have put on the new man, which is renewed in knowledge after the image of him that created him: ¹¹ Where there is neither Greek nor Jew, circumcision nor uncircumcision, Barbarian, Scythian, bond nor free: but Christ is all, and in all.

¹² Put on therefore, as the elect of God, holy and beloved, bowels of mercies, kindness, humbleness of mind, meekness, longsuffering;

¹³ Forbearing one another, and forgiving one another, if any man have a quarrel against any: even as Christ forgave you, so also do ye. ¹⁴ And above all these things put on charity, which is the bond of perfectness.

¹⁵And let the peace of God rule in your hearts, to the which also ye are called in one body; and be ye thankful. ¹⁶ Let the word of Christ dwell in you richly in all wisdom; teaching and admonishing one another in psalms and hymns and spiritual songs, singing with grace in your hearts to the Lord. ¹⁷ And whatsoever ye do in word or deed, do all in the name of the Lord Jesus, giving thanks to God and the Father by him.

Recessional

Recessional

While the music chosen for the entrance of the bride may be solemn or reflective, the music used as the bridal party exits the wedding venue should emulate the joyous celebration of the marriage that has taken place, and as such a spirited piece of classical music is the perfect choice.

Bearing this in mind, it is not unusual for "The Arrival Of The Queen Of Sheba" to be used as a recessional piece rather than a processional despite its title.

Alternatively, you could opt for a classic pop song such as "All You Need Is Love," performed by a gospel choir in the film *Love, Actually*; or Abba's lyrically suitable "I Do, I Do, I Do, I Do, I Do."

The timings for the recessional will be similar to that of the processional; note however that the exit music should start as the bride and groom are ready to leave the venue. It doesn't matter if the music plays on after they have left, indeed, a longer work may well continue for several minutes afterward. Guests will also start to leave by this point and it may be that postlude music is almost unnecessary.

An organ or piano will probably accompany the recessional, although, as per other parts of the service, a string quartet, wind ensemble or gospel choir would also work well.

The Arrival Of The Queen Of Sheba - Handel 194
Hallelujah Chorus from "The Messiah" - Handel 189
Overture To The Marriage Of Figaro - Mozart 198
La Rejouissance from "Music For The Royal Fireworks" - Handel 202
Toccata from Symphony No. 5 - Widor 204
Wedding March from "A Midsummer Night's Dream" - Mendelssohn 208
All You Need Is Love (as used in *Love, Actually*) - The Beatles 214
I Do, I Do, I Do, I Do, I Do (as used in *Mamma Mia!*) - Abba 218

Other suggestions:
Signed, Sealed, Delivered - Stevie Wonder
I'm Yours - Jason Mraz

Refer to the Processional chapter for further suggestions.

Hallelujah Chorus

from "The Messiah"

Composed by George Frideric Handel

The Arrival Of The Queen Of Sheba

Composed by George Frideric Handel

Overture To The Marriage Of Figaro

Composed by Wolfgang Amadeus Mozart

La Rejouissance

from "Music For The Royal Fireworks"

Composed by George Frederic Handel

Toccata
from Symphony No. 5

Composed by Charles-Marie Widor

Wedding March
from "A Midsummer Night's Dream"

Composed by Felix Mendelssohn

All You Need Is Love

Words & Music by John Lennon & Paul McCartney

215

I Do, I Do, I Do, I Do, I Do

Words & Music by Benny Andersson, Björn Ulvaeus & Stig Anderson

Postlude

Postlude

The brief for the music to played as your guests leave the wedding venue is largely the same as that of the *Prelude*. However, your guests will probably be a lot more animated and thus chattier now than they were before the ceremony and as such livelier and more energetic pieces should be chosen to reflect this.

Ten minutes of music after the service ends is probably sufficient, and again this could be provided by the organist, pianist or another instrumental or vocal ensemble.

Although the suggestions included in this chapter are all classical pieces, do not feel limited to this genre.

Jesu, Joy Of Man's Desiring

Composed by Johann Sebastian Bach

Moderato, poco allegretto

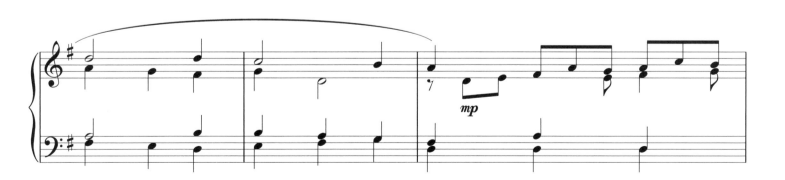

poco rall.

Salut D'Amour

Music by Sir Edward Elgar

Spring
from "The Four Seasons"
1st Movement

Composed by Antonio Vivaldi

Winter

from "The Four Seasons"

2nd Movement

Composed by Antonio Vivaldi

Reception & First Dance

Reception & First Dance

Choosing music beyond the ceremony itself is a much less-structured process, dependant entirely upon the format of your wedding day.

You may wish to provide music as guests arrive at the reception venue or as background music during a meal. A string or wind ensemble are favored choices for this, although their repertoire need not be limited to classical. A solo pianist or harpist are also interesting options.

If you are planning to incorporate a "disco" element into your day, you will need to decide whether to use a live band or a DJ. If booking a live band, consider what style of music you want—jazz, swing, rock or pop. Both bands and DJs will probably have a song list spanning a huge variety of music, and you should be able to guide them to the particular genre you like best, be it '70s disco or retro synth-laden '80s pop.

While there is an enormous degree of variation in the format of a wedding day after the ceremony itself, a few aspects remain constant, and the first dance of the bride and groom is one of these. First and foremost you should choose a song that both of you like. If there is a particular song that is special to you as a couple, use that; it doesn't need to be a love song. It could be something timeless such as The Carpenters, or contemporary such as Robbie Williams; a classic pop ballad such as "Wonderful Tonight" or an up-tempo jazz number such as "Fly Me To The Moon." Perhaps there is a song from a film that you have watched many times together, such as Bryan Adams's "(Everything I Do) I Do It For You" from *Robin Hood, Prince Of Thieves* or Aerosmith's rock ballad "I Don't Want To Miss A Thing" from *Armageddon.*

Do not worry about the "dance" element; your guests will not be expecting a choreographed routine! Instead, pick something you are comfortable with. Another great idea, however, is to use a classical dance such as a waltz or polka, at which point knowing the steps would be very impressive.

A recording of the song could be played through a PA system—particularly straightforward if you are using a DJ for a disco element of your day—or you could ask someone to perform the song live. If you are using a live band for a disco, they should be happy to do this, provided that you give them plenty of notice. Alternatively, this could be another opportunity to include a musically-talented friend in the proceedings. The backing tracks included with this book could be especially useful in this instance as it is unlikely that there will be a piano or other accompanying instrument at the reception venue.

Other suggestions:

Crazy Little Thing Called Love - Queen

Nobody Does It Better - Carly Simon

When A Man Loves A Woman - Percy Sledge

(Everything I Do) I Do It For You

Words and Music by Bryan Adams, Robert John "Mutt" Lange & Michael Kamen

Original key D♭ major

𝅘𝅥 = 80

2.

Oh, you can't tell me it's not worth try - in' for. I can't
help__ it, there's noth-ing I want more.__ Yeah, I would fight for you,_ I'd_
lie_____ for you,___ walk the wire for you,___ yeah,_ I'd
die for___ you.___ You know it's true, ev - 'ry - thing I___

Play 8 times ad lib. and fade

255

Fly Me To The Moon

Words & Music by Bart Howard

oth-er words,___ please be true,___ in

oth-er words_____ I___ love you.

I Don't Want To Miss A Thing

Words & Music by Diane Warren

smile while you are sleep - ing,___ while you're far a - way___ and dream - ing. I could

spend my life___ in this sweet sur - ren - der. I could

stay lost in this mo - ment for - ev - er. Ev - 'ry mo - ment

spent with___ you___ is a mo - ment I treas - ure.

Don't wan-na close my eyes, I don't wan-na fall a - sleep, 'cause I'd

miss you, ba - by, and I don't wan-na miss a thing. 'Cause e - ven when I dream of you,

the sweet-est dream would nev - er do; I'd still miss you, ba - by, and I don't wan-na miss a thing.

2. Ly - ing

D.S. al Coda

close to you,__ feel-ing your__ heart beat - ing, and I'm won - d'ring what you're dream-ing, won-d'ring if it's me you're see - ing. Then I kiss your eyes__ and thank God we're to-geth - er.__ I just wan-na stay with you__ in this mo-ment for - ev - er,__ for-ev - er and ev - er.__

And I don't wan-na miss one smile;_____ and I don't wan-na

miss one kiss.   I just wan-na be with you,__ right here__ with you,__

just like this.   I just wan-na hold__ you close,_____ I feel your heart so

close to mine,_____   and just stay here in__ this mo-ment for all the

I don't wan-na close my eyes, I don't wan-na fall a - sleep, 'cause I'd

miss you, ba - by, and I don't wan-na miss a thing. 'Cause e - ven when I dream of you,

the sweet-est dream would nev - er do; I'd still miss you, ba - by, and I don't wan-na miss a thing.

Repeat and fade

ad lib. vocal

She's The One

Words & Music by Karl Wallinger

Someone Like You

Words & Music by Van Morrison

Wonderful Tonight

Words & Music by Eric Clapton

won - der_____ of it all_____ is that you just don't_ re - al - ize_

___ how much_ I love___ you.

D.S. al Coda

We've Only Just Begun

Words & Music by Roger Nichols & Paul Williams

a kiss for luck_ and we've on our_ way._

(We've on - ly__ be-

-gun.)

2. Be - fore__ the ris - ing sun_____ we

3, 4. And, when__ the eve - ning comes,_____ we

fly;_____

smile;_____

so man - y roads to choose,____

so much of life a - head,____

we start out walk - ing and learn to__ run.__

we'll find a place_ where there's room to__ grow.

To Coda

(And yes, we've just be-gun.)

Shar-ing ho-ri - zons that are new to us,

watch-ing the signs_ a - long_ the way._

Talk-ing it o - ver, just the two_ of us;

working to-geth-er day__ to day,__ to-

1. - geth-er.__

2. - geth-er,__ to - geth-er.__

D.S. al Coda

Coda

And yes, we've just be-gun.__

The Music You Chose

Processional

....

Hymns and Readings

....
....
....
....
....

Signing Of The Register

....

Recessional

....

First Dance

....

INDEX

DISC 1

1. Air from "The Water Music"
   (Handel)
2. Ave Verum Corpus, K618
   (Mozart)
3. Minuet from "String Quartet"
   (Boccherini)
4. Sheep May Safely Graze
   (Bach)
5. Everybody's Free (To Feel Good)
   (Swanston/Cox)
6. Bridal Chorus from "Lohengrin"
   (Wagner)
7. Gloria from "Gloria"
   (Vivaldi)
8. Hornpipe from "Water Music"
   (Handel)
9. Prelude To Te Deum
   (Charpentier)
10. Trumpet Tune
    (Purcell)
11. Trumpet Voluntary
    (Clarke)
12. Wedding Processional
    (Rodgers)
13. All Things Bright And Beautiful
    (Traditional/Shaw/Alexander)
14. Amazing Grace
    (Newton)
15. Dear Lord And Father Of Mankind
    (Greenleaf Whittier/Maker)
16. Guide Me, O Thou Great Redeemer
    (Williams/Hughes)
17. Jerusalem
    (Parry)
18. Lord Of All Hopefullness
    (Traditional/Struther)
19. Love Divine, All Loves Excelling
    (Wesley/Rowlands)
20. Praise, My Soul, The King Of Heaven
    (Lyte/Goss)

DISC 2

1. Gymnopédie No. 1
   (Satie)
2. Ave Maria
   (Schubert)
3. Panis Angelicus
   (Franck)
4. Come What May
   (Baerwald)
5. From This Moment On
   (Twain/Lange)
6. I Swear
   (Baker/Myers)
7. My Love
   (McCartney/McCartney)
8. Suddenly
   (Anderson/Cichon/Beamish)
9. Up Where We Belong
   (Jennings/Sainte-Marie/Nitzsche)
10. You Take My Breath Away
    (Hamill)
11. Hallelujah Chorus from "The Messiah"
    (Handel)
12. The Arrival Of The Queen Of Sheba
    (Handel)
13. Overture To The Marriage Of Figaro
    (Mozart)
14. La Rejouissance from "Music For The Royal Fireworks"
    (Handel)
15. Toccata from Symphony No. 5
    (Widor)
16. Wedding March from "A Midsummer Night's Dream"
    (Mendelssohn)
17. All You Need Is Love
    (Lennon/McCartney)
18. I Do, I Do, I Do, I Do, I Do
    (Andersson/Ulvaeus/Anderson)

DISC 3

1. Jesu, Joy Of Man's Desiring
   (Bach)
2. Salut D'Amour
   (Elgar)
3. Spring from "The Four Seasons" (1st Movement)
   (Vivaldi)
4. Winter from "The Four Seasons" (2nd Movement)
   (Vivaldi)
5. (Everything I Do) I Do It For You
   (Adams/Lange/Kamen)
6. Fly Me To The Moon (In Other Words)
   (Howard)
7. I Don't Want To Miss A Thing
   (Warren)
8. She's The One
   (Wallinger)
9. Someone Like You
   (Morrison)
10. Wonderful Tonight
    (Clapton)
11. We've Only Just Begun
    (Nichols/Williams)

To remove your CD from the plastic sleeve,
lift the small lip to break the perforations.
Replace the disc after use for convenient storage.